penguin life

home

whitney hanson is excited to share *home*, her first collection of poetry, with her readers. whitney is a twenty-year-old university student who believes that sharing one's story is the key to impacting others. she deeply believes that pain can be converted to purpose. she hopes that you will find the purpose for your pain in the pages of her book, and she ultimately aims to help her readers "make peace with their bees."

h⬡me

whitney hanson

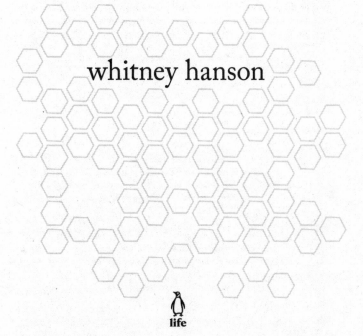

life

PENGUIN BOOKS
An imprint of Penguin Random House LLC
penguinrandomhouse.com

First self-published in the United States of America 2021
Published with an introduction and additional poems in Penguin Books 2023

A Penguin Life Book

LIBRARY OF CONGRESS CATALOGING-IN-PUBLICATION DATA
Names: Hanson, Whitney, author.
Title: Home / Whitney Hanson.
Other titles: Home (Compilation)
Description: New York: Penguin Life, 2023.
Identifiers: LCCN 2023001298 (print) | LCCN 2023001299 (ebook) |
ISBN 9780143138006 (paperback) | ISBN 9780593512098 (ebook)
Subjects: LCGFT: Poetry.
Classification: LCC PS3608.A72336 H66 2023 (print) |
LCC PS3608.A72336 (ebook) | DDC 811/6—dc23/eng/20230117
LC record available at https://lccn.loc.gov/2023001298
LC ebook record available at https://lccn.loc.gov/2023001299

Printed in the United States of America
6th Printing

Set in Adobe Caslon Pro • Designed by Sabrina Bowers

for those who have loved me, hurt me,
and healed me

contents

introduction

the other day, someone asked me "why did you decide to write a book?"

i would like to say i had an altruistic mission to save the world from heartbreak, but the truth is, writing this book was primarily an act of saving myself.

when i began writing *home*, i was in my sophomore year of college. i was lost in almost every area of life. covid had derailed my freshman experience and my sophomore year was shaping up to be no less chaotic. i was a student athlete who was struggling with the pressure of athletics. i was unsure about the direction of my academic future. my romantic relationships had left me heartbroken and questioning my worth. as a result of all this, i was in the lowest place i had ever been mentally and emotionally. i knew that something needed to change, but sometimes when you have a powerful emotional experience involving specific people or specific places, you develop an attachment to those people and locations. it takes a lot of bravery to leave relationships behind even when you know it is best for you. i was overwhelmed with heartbreak, confusion, anxiety, and loss.

my mind and heart were flooded with those bees.

writing became my only way to calm them down.

as i wrote, all the words spilled out: the ones i wanted to say to the people who loved me then left me, the ones i used to save myself when i felt lonelier than i ever have. i even wrote down the words that i simply wanted to scream into the void on my darkest nights.

one of the most difficult realities about heartbreak is that it is never going to disappear from you entirely. some days you will find peace, on others the bees will swarm your mind and sting you from the inside. they serve as a reminder that love does not exit the room gracefully.

through writing *home*, i found that healing isn't a process of vanquishing the bees. it's a process of making peace with the bees. it's a journey of acceptance and reorienting the heart, of finding home within yourself. if there is a message i could convey through my journey, it is that it is never too late to leave. it is never too late to start defining your identity on your own terms. it is never too late to begin your journey home.

despite my fear and sadness, i did what i needed to do. i left and began my journey home. i relocated physically, to a new city, in a new state, 1,842 miles away from my hometown. and i sent out this collection of my pain and healing like a cry into the universe.

i never thought anyone would hear me. i never imagined anyone would understand. but to my surprise, this voice replied. it was yours. quiet at first. then gradually louder. finally, i was overwhelmed by the sea of people crying back from the emptiness, "me too." those two words brought me the hope i never knew i needed.

so now i give my story to you and i hope that somewhere in these pages you discover pieces of your heart. i hope that you use this book like a road map home when the world around you feels dark. most of all i hope that despite how impossible it seems, someday you find a way to make peace with your bees.

losing

i remember the last night i spent in your room
i've never really liked people touching me
but something about the way you always
smelled like honey
and how you held me without hesitation
made it easy for me to find comfort in touch again

i remember the last night i spent in your room
you told me that you slept with her
my skin began to crawl
and somehow honey
started to smell like danger
you became a beehive
bursting with everything i was afraid of

i remember the last night i spent in your room
i'm not sure why i didn't run
when the bees filled my head
and venom stung in my veins
and you tried to hold on to me
but all i felt was poignant pain

i remember the last night i spent in your room
i've never really liked people touching me
and something about the way your honey
turned into venom
and how there are bees in my brain
makes me hope that no one ever touches me again

you're not who i thought you were

"maybe it was love"
she casts doubt into my dim bedroom

"they don't mean to hurt you, you're just difficult to
love"

"they are treating you this way because you deserve it"

"they just want what is best for you, you're making
this up in your mind"

"they slept with another girl, but it's probably because of
something you didn't give them"

she doesn't always make sense
but sometimes she's awfully convincing
~*the voice inside my head*

love letters i've received:
i want you
but not right now

she loves me
she loves me not

i've been tossing flower petals to the wind
hoping that one of them reaches you
but my questions are always met with confusion

she loves me
she loves me not

i keep counting
calculating
circling around your words
searching for an i love you
between your kindness and inconsistency

she loves me
she loves me not

i chase your heart around daisies
the same way i count the seconds on the clock
waiting for you to call

she loves me
she loves me not

i am tired of playing games for your love
i am tired of asking flowers for answers
but right now, flowers are all that i've got
because she won't tell me

if she loves me
or loves me not

dear empathy,
please stop telling me
that it's okay when they hurt me
stop allowing me to accept
the knife you see in their side
is a reasonable excuse
for them to put two in mine
please stop introducing me to their demons
i don't want to shake hands
with the reasons
they can't seem to stay
please stop waving a white flag
and making me pity their anger
and make peace with their madness

exhausted from a culture of
i love you for tonight
but tomorrow it may be different

and let me borrow the parts of you
that i need to make me whole
but never take all of you

in a world where the word commitment
tastes like poison
in our mouths

please tell me
why is it so difficult for someone to stay?

i want to exist in a world
where love isn't an emotion
it is a promise

where i love you for tonight
means i will be there tomorrow

and where you borrow the parts of me
that you need to make you whole
along with all the rest

where commitment doesn't taste so bitter

please tell me
it isn't so difficult to stay

i don't care
is what i said

but i meant it in the way flowers
pretend not to care about the winter snow
they stand there frozen
unaffected
but as soon as the snow melts away
they fall to pieces
petal by petal they surrender to the cold

i don't care
is what i said

but i wilted as soon as you turned your head
all my hope fell like petals to the floor
along with every i love you i ever said

i don't care is
what i said

but inside me
something once alive
was now dead

hold my breath and count to ten
one two three
forget how your hands might look on her skin
five six seven
eight reasons that you can't be upset so stop
nine ten eleven
twelve i was supposed to exhale at ten
thirteen fourteen fifteen
sixteen maybe it takes more than ten seconds
to let it go

if it's not meant to be
tell my why her sweatshirt smells like comfort

if it's not meant to be
tell me why i'm flooded with hurt but
the minute i see her my heart melts

if it's not meant to be
tell me why she plays on repeat
like a song in my head
and i don't want to press pause

if it's not meant to be
tell me why i can't stop
retracing her body in my mind

if it's not meant to be
tell me why the person i am with her
is who i want to be

if it's not meant to be
tell me why

stop making excuses for their behavior

i stand here fully dressed
to say goodbye
but you left me naked
embarrassed of all i showed you
clothing can only keep you as safe
as the walls you put around your heart
i took my walls down for you
i wish i hadn't

what hurts the most
are memories we didn't make
the pictures i had of our future
i spent an eternity waking up to you
tell me,
how do i forget things that never happened?

eventually they're not going to be
your person anymore
they won't be the one
you want to share sunsets and shooting stars with
they won't be the one
you want to call when your feelings
are too heavy to carry alone
i know that right now you want to run to them
but closed arms will not hold you
and careless hearts will not heal you

i have a bad habit
of clinging to the people and places
that have been hurting me
today i asked myself to explain why
because sometimes
it doesn't make sense to me either
this is the conclusion i have come to
i stay because although i'm treated poorly
i find comfort in the surety
of knowing exactly what i'm getting.
moving on is a commitment to uncertainty
and things could always be worse
on the other side of a big jump

i have never been good with risk
i don't like to gamble
i like control

when i heard you found someone new
my blood became
liquid concrete in my veins
angry and shaking i cut open my skin
hoping i could pull you out
but instead, the concrete began to harden
i think it is better that way
maybe i was meant to be a statue
a stone-cold depiction of
all the reasons
you shouldn't fall in love
a reminder of the damage
that people with
dark eyes and enticing smiles can do
and i hope that that someone you found
finds my statue too
before it's too late for them
to walk away from you

~*statue*

change is scary
you're going to be okay

don't stay because you're comfortable
this is not your home

i gave your sweatshirt back today
it won't go down as a historic event
one hundred years from now
no one will care that it happened
no one will even know
and that's what i have to think about
to make it feel okay

sometimes the battles
that take the most strength
are the ones you choose
not to fight
~surrender

at some point
i stopped writing you poems
hoping that you'd fall in love
and i started writing about
how it felt when you didn't

i bought a candle that i didn't need
i already have a perfectly good candle at home
but for some reason
i bought another one
i think i have a tendency to prepare to lose things
before they are gone

it is never selfish to take care of your heart. if you need to move, then move. if you need to stay, then stay. don't let anyone else dictate where your peace lands.

i know that we are no good for each other
i know that you have not been good to me
but still somewhere in you
i found a piece of myself
all this time
i thought i was the only one whose soul danced
to this music
then i found that yours did too
it's hard to move on my own again

kiss me one more time before we lose our minds

prove to me that love is a verb
let your actions speak for how you feel
and if they are not loud
let me leave

kisses like candle wax
you give them
and i peel them off
because your love
burns my skin

last time i kiss you
last time i sleep with your head in the space
between my heart and my chin
last time you hold me when i'm hurt
last time your skin feels like home
last time you are my person
last time i am capable of loving someone this way

why did you have to ruin something so good?

sometimes
caring
is
a
curse

loving you
felt like leaving a book out in the wind
the pages turned too fast for me to read
i didn't get enough time
to adore you
to explore you
to trace your lines with my fingertips
and reread my favorite parts
to live the story i knew we were meant to be
before i knew it
the book was closed
the story was over
~unfinished

people with the most intricate minds
have the most turmoil inside
you cannot be filled with the galaxies
and not expect explosions

you loved me for my mind
you left me for my mind

we both know that want and need
are too different words
but somehow we keep getting them mixed up

i know this is not what i need
but i want you anyway

i knew for months that she was sleeping
in someone else's bed
why then did it take me so long to leave?

i was not surprised
you play defensively
like me
reserving your pieces
not willing to make sacrifices
that is why the game took so long
neither of us willing
to give up what we wanted
i think that's why
you and i
didn't work
~love authored by chess

sometimes there is nothing poetic
about the way it hurts
sometimes it just hurts
that's okay

i know that if you knew how you are making me feel
you'd walk away forever
and that is why i have to pretend
that i'm okay with this

if you're like me, you struggle with walking away from situations that aren't healthy for you. if you're like me, it is hard to see the line between i care for you and i will put your needs before mine until my feet are blistered from racing to catch you every time you fall. if you are like me, then listen. walking away from situations that are hurting you does not mean that you are heartless. it means that you have outgrown the shoes you've been using to chase unreciprocated love. it means that you are learning to value yourself. you have not lost your capacity for love. you are discovering how to love you.

when i found out you slept with someone else
i stayed up until 3 a.m. painting a portrait of you
when you ignored me for weeks
i bought you a guitar and left it in your room
i've realized that sometimes
you can't resurrect broken relationships
with kindness

i don't think you understand how many times i've had to do this. the first person that i loved broke my heart six times. every time he asked for me back. i was there with my arms open. a heart with three different cracks has the same capacity for love, right? the second person i loved, loved me for a month. the next year, he spent making sure he showed me only enough love that i would stay. he walked as close as he could to the line without crossing it. finally, there's you. you had me convinced that you were my safe place. that maybe i was enough for someone. until enough became something you found between another girl's thighs. and still i stay. because i remain who i've always been. and maybe it's me. i have never been the one that is strong enough to walk away when i am not wanted. i would rather stay with a broken heart than leave and be whole.

she could feel the ending before it came. like a book that's almost finished, she was counting down the pages she had left. she cried every time she had to turn the page.

don't doubt your ability to move forward. even as you read these words you are making progress, moving toward a destination. it is as easy as tracing these lines with your eyes. a little at a time.

you

will

find

the

new

you

i know this feeling is familiar for you now
you're getting used to letting go
knowing they're the only one you want to talk to
but not being able to go to them
beginning to realize that even if you did go back
it wouldn't be the same
their heart has changed
believe it or not so has yours
this is only the beginning of the end
but you have done this before
you are stronger than you know

i don't know how to love small
so if i can't love you a lot
i can't love you at all

my happiness is the rent i pay for staying here

my wallet is empty now

there isn't anything redeemable

about promising you will be there

then not showing up

you closed your eyes
because you didn't want to see

you are brave enough to hurt me
but not brave enough to watch me bleed

i found a list in my notes of things that i wanted to know about you when we met. i wish i could unlearn those things now.

sometimes i close my eyes
and picture myself getting undressed
first, i shave off all my hair
if you want to run your fingers through it again
it's on the floor where you left my heart
next, i peel off my skin
i cannot keep anything your hands have touched
then, i pull out my eyes
maybe it is better not to know sight
than to see you moving on
one by one i pull out my teeth
and throw them
i have to get those three words i said
far far far away
finally, when i am entirely naked of you
i cry
i water the ground
and hope that something new
grows at my feet

i think i am the kind of person
who people fall in love with
too quickly
and i don't mean to complain
because it is wonderful to be loved
but i am also the kind of person
who people walk away from
when they realize
the beautiful pool of water
that they wandered into
is actually an ocean
with too many questions
i wish my company
didn't make people feel
like they're drowning
mystery draws them in
then mystery makes them leave

i'm not a hopeless romantic
i only want romance when it's gone
i am hopeless
but not because i long for love
i am hopeless
because i never know how
to appreciate you
when you're mine

when you're with me you love me
when you're with her you love her

i don't need you to explain
why we don't work
that won't ease the frustration
i feel every time your name
comes up on my phone
i need you to explain
why you won't try
why trying isn't worth it to you
i need you to explain
why occasionally you take interest in my life
is it just to keep me hoping?

i spend my days reminding myself that you don't care
i spend my nights dreaming that you still do

you don't have commitment issues
i know that you think you do
but you must realize
not committing
is simply committing to something else
every commitment
has a counter commitment
if you don't jump into the river
you are committing to stay on land
you are not afraid of commitment
you are afraid to take a risk
you are afraid to drown
i hope you find what you are looking for on land

i love you isn't currency
to get you what you want
my body is not an experiment
to fill your empty spots
i am not your pawn
and this is not a game
it's just something you did wrong
i'm your mistake

walking away
means having the strength to say
this is no longer my problem

leave and watch them
fall in love with someone else
stay and fail to receive
the love you deserve
~pick your poison

home

losing you isn't just losing you
it is losing the me that i was with you
i'm going to miss her

if they are not choosing you
it is not love
if you are not a priority
it is not love
if you have to ask
"is this love?"
it is not love

ice cream with my ex

"you'll always have a soft spot for me," she teased

"that's not funny," i replied, holding back tears from my eyes
and knowing she was right

there are all these words piling up
straining and staining these pages
with emotions i can no longer share
i am longing to tell you
but my tongue remains chained
by your impervious demeanor
you are not the same
even if i let my words loose
they wouldn't get through
so i remain silent
~talking to a brick wall

i still can't help feeling
like i was supposed to love you forever
~denial

kiss me
before you go kiss her
remind me i'm beautiful
just to admire someone else
keep me here
just in case
~false reassurance

you're sleeping next to me
and i'm not sure what to do
i do not know how to wake you
if not with a kiss on the forehead
but you are not mine to kiss
so i guess i will let you sleep

when i packed up and left
i sobbed the 377 miles i drove away
this reminded me that just because
leaving is the right thing to do
that doesn't make it easy

home

real love
doesn't use your love
as a weapon
against you

i pierced my ear and it got infected
for weeks my ear was red and swollen
i knew that if i just took the earring out
i could heal much faster
but i thought the earring
made me feel beautiful
so i let it stay
~toxic relationships

i learned to hold on tightly to people when death stole my best friend at age 15. suddenly, i'm 20 years old and my knuckles are still white from refusing to let go of love.

~attachment issues

i want to be someone you can't stay away from
i want to be like your bed in the morning
it takes everything to leave its warmth
and at the end of the day, you always return
i want to be comfort

i realize that i'm someone
you need to stay away from
i realize that i am more like a fire
you want to get close
but i keep burning you
i am your destruction
and i hate that

coming to terms with betrayal
is a funny thing

i know now that i am not wounded
because you hurt me
i am hurt
because i love you

i am not dead
because you killed me
i am dead
because i thought you would save me
and you didn't

i'm not very good at taking criticism. i know you weren't criticizing me when you decided to be with her. but it feels like everything you give to her that you couldn't give to me is a testament of my faults. i imagine you kiss lines down her body that spell out all of the reasons i am unlovable.

when you are asleep, i can pretend that you are still the person you used to be. your breath still moves in and out like ocean tides, calming and consistent. you still smell like honey and your hair still falls in soft piles onto the pillow. your lips are still the ones that told me you would stay and the way you twitch as you fall deeper asleep reminds me that somehow you are the same. i can pretend not to know that in your chest your heart beats for her and not for me.

to be clear
loving her was not the mistake
staying when she didn't love you was

how dare you
make me promises
you couldn't keep

lost

the bees are still in my head

someday
i will have poured all of the memories
out of my eyes
and when my mind searches for you
all it will find
is a dried-up garden
that has gone so long
without water
that i no longer remember
what it looked like
in full bloom

home

you didn't break my heart
you shattered it into a million pieces
you hid those pieces

i can't find them

i can't find myself

it's okay
make me hurt
the finest art
is painted
with the blood
of a broken heart

it's as if i'm stuck between breaths
wedged in the moment between
the inhale and the exhale
filled to capacity
cursed with the inability
to let it all go

i wish you knew that it takes everything i have to keep it together around you

the sad part
is that i can write a thousand lines
about the way you broke me
and it won't put me back together
and it won't bring you back

there is no good reason to go back to people who did not choose you. do not put your heart in the hands of someone who doesn't want to hold it.

she didn't choose you
and as hard as it is
that means you must stop choosing her
~*hard truths*

when i say i miss being happy
i really mean i miss you
because somewhere along the way
those two words became synonymous

i mark my place in the poetry book you gave me with the polaroid we took the last time i told you that i loved you.

maybe if i can hide us between pages covered in lovely words, maybe if i surround us with raw emotion, maybe then what we were will never die.

i fell in love with you in the fall
and perhaps that was my mistake
i failed to realize
that fall leads to winter
and winter is lonely and cold
next time
can we fall in love
in the spring?

i hate when i can feel time going by. when i lost you, i could sense every second lengthening the gap between who we used to be and who we are becoming. i bet you didn't know it's been 31,350 minutes since the last time i kissed you. i hope you didn't know that. i hope time has been kinder to you than it has to me.

it is interesting
the ways i will betray myself
to love you

it is torture that
the narrator in my mind
seems to be on your side

it is fatal
that i know i would follow you
to the end of myself

waking up in the morning
is the hardest part about losing someone
something about sleep
convinces you that
you'll wake up with a fresh start
but every morning i wake up
and remember you're gone

~*a.m.*

sometimes when i go to bed
before i turn out the light
i take my heavy heart out
and put it away for the night
so if in the morning
you do not see me rise
it's because i can't seem to put it back
without putting tears in my eyes

~*p.m.*

seeing you hurts
not seeing you hurts too
~*paradox*

i am both
too much
and never enough

i am like the ocean
all the water you could ever need
but i am salt water
and you were looking for a drink

sometimes when it's cold outside
i like to sit in it
until my outsides match my insides
~*numb*

i cleaned you out of my car today
i needed to remember
that my passenger seat
is no longer reserved for you
i threw away the empty ice cream cups
from when we used to go for late night
ice cream and talk
i removed the rubber duck
from my dashboard
you should understand why
i changed the playlist
that i listen to when i drive
i rolled down the windows
hoped that it would air out my heart
and i drove away

home

sometimes you aren't ready to unpack and that's okay.
sometimes you just want to hold hostage the way she loved
you once as if someone may come along and repay you for all
of the heartache you spent on her.

sometimes you have to let the hostage go without reparations.

103

when you lose her, for the first time in months, you will sleep alone.

your blankets will stop smelling like her, and when you reach out in the middle of the night, her hand won't be reaching back.

you will not fall asleep with your fingers tangled, one in her hand and the other in her hair. your hands will be empty. empty.

you will throw the extra pillow on your bed across the room because every time you look at it you're sure she will be there.

you will stare at the ceiling with the same eyes that used to get lost in hers and it won't matter how many blankets you put on. you will be cold.

you will question why she didn't choose you and you'll wonder who she is sleeping with now because you know she can't sleep alone.

you will breathe, reach, tangle your fingers in your sheets, stare into nowhere and cry. and then finally, you will let go.

for the first time in months, you will become accustomed to sleeping alone.

doubt keeps telling me that i made the wrong choice
that i will never find a love like this one
that this is the only place that i will feel at home

you are not a second choice
they didn't choose you
not because you are not worthy
but because they weren't built to love you

i know their arms
feel like they were supposed to carry you
but their lack of strength
is not a testimony of the weight of your soul
but rather the weakness of theirs
you are not too much

it feels like you're lost. you're on a ship sailing through troubled waters, occasionally pulling a drowning soul on board. you mend whatever has left them broken. once they are whole, they leave, and you are alone again. sometimes you want to jump overboard and let someone save you instead. but you are too kind to be a temporary passenger in someone's heart.

do me a favor.

stay on board.

you're not lost you are finding.

i can feel abandonment crawling through my veins and every time i think of how you told me you wouldn't leave, i have to pull off a layer of skin to escape the grip of your lying hands on my body.

today i was envious of a goldfish
somewhere i heard
that goldfish have a memory
that lasts three seconds
i would spend the rest of my life
in a fishbowl
to forget the way it felt to hold you

there is no "appropriate" way to grieve
light things on fire
or don't

it isn't just that i didn't matter to you
it's that this will be another case
in the file cabinet in my mind
to prove my hypothesis
that i don't matter at all
and the file is getting too big
and my heart is feeling awfully small
and i can't help but wish
that you would have proved me wrong

i want to take a knife and peel myself like an orange. i want to pick out all the parts that no one wants and throw them away.

home

she seems nice but
please don't tell me about
the little things she does to make you laugh
please don't post videos
of her dancing around her room
please don't walk around
holding her hand and looking into her soul
because i have a sense of humor too
and i can dance around the room
i have hands to hold and a soul to see
she's seems nice but
you doing those things with her
reminds me that you're not doing them with me

she seems nice but
please don't tell me about
the little things she does to make you laugh
please don't post videos
of her dancing around her room
please don't walk around
holding her hand and looking into her soul
because i have a sense of humor too
and i can dance around the room
i have hands to hold and a soul to see
she's seems nice but
you doing those things with her
reminds me that you're not doing them with me

when i'm hurting, i have a tendency to shove myself into small places. usually, i get in my closet and sit in the dark. it's like if i can squeeze all of my pain into a tiny place maybe i can make it feel a little smaller.

i can't go outside
i'm too scared i'm going to run into you with her

you've just come in from a rainstorm
you can't expect to be
immediately dry warm and comfortable
but you can do the little things
take off the heavy clothing
turn on the coffee pot
wrap yourself in a blanket
one small thing at a time
~healing is a process

i hate you flower
i hate the way that nature gives you all you need
i needed her
and now i'm alone

you always said you got motion sickness
i guess that's why i'm confused
that you're the one who moved on so quickly
and i'm heaving up memories from my stomach
trying to get a grip on the ground

you always said you got motion sickness
but i don't think that's what you mean
i don't think you're sick of moving
you're just sick of me

i ache for the music your heart made with mine

sometimes it hurts so bad that you shake and tears stream down your face and each inhale feels like a battle between you and the world that is collapsing around you.

~panic

sometimes it hurts so bad that you can't move. you stay in your bed for days and stare and the ceiling. you lose the line between you and everything else in the world.

~paralysis

i've been staring at myself
i keep wishing that i could find
the reason that you left in my mirror
sometimes i think it's in the shape of my nose
or in my untamable hair
but you always told me you adored those things
so, if on the outside, i am enough for you
if i can't find the reason you left in my mirror
then it must be inside of me
that is my greatest fear
~*reflection*

whitney hanson

i love to read books
they are safe
if the plot becomes too messy
i can simply close the book
i wish i could trap my life
in the pages of a book

home

please don't tell me that my space in your heart
belongs to someone new

you are music
constantly fighting its way into my mind
a violent, rebellious, but beautiful melody
i try to turn down the volume
i try anything to turn down the volume
i fight
i talk
i write
i paint
i submerge my head in water and i scream
why won't you get out of my head?

as much as you would like them to be
apologies are not always bandages
to mend a broken heart

sometimes i'm a rain-soaked pile strewn across my unmade bed. every movement carries the weight of a thousand storm clouds. i am waiting for someone to pick me up and wring me out but every time they try, i scream. their hands attempting to twist me and remove the heaviness. they don't know that the heaviness keeps me safe. losing all of this water means losing control. leaving my bed is a risk i'm not willing to take.

i know this is my fault too

~*guilty*

cleaning makes me feel like I have control
as if manipulating the area around me
will somehow rearrange whatever is broken within me
as if removing the speckles from my mirror
will somehow clarify
all of the *whys* that are eating me alive
am i so far gone that folding my socks
makes it easier to breath?
the irony
that i love when everything has a place
and at the same time feel that
i have no place here

home

i author my own chaos
then ask why the tempest won't subside

i am an expert at appreciating everything about her.
why can't i love me that way?

i think you loved me more than you knew me

that is to say
that you wanted to love me
more than you were capable of loving me

you wanted someone's chest to rest your heart on
more than you wanted to know the depths
of the person that held you

it isn't a crime not to love someone wholly
but sometimes i wish it were
because to be loved in halves
seems heavier than an ocean of loneliness

to be loved and not known
is almost worse than never to be loved at all

i've always liked my own company
but now when i'm alone
your words are all that i hear

so here i sit in public places
hoping that the voices around me
will be louder than the voices within

home

i take pride in my impressive vocabulary
so why is your name the only word that comes out of my
mouth these days?
this is getting old

what if no one wants to read it?
what if no one else feels this way?
what if you're just obsessive?
~self-criticism

home

my friends keep telling me
that you weren't that special
and that i will find someone new
but they didn't see the way your body wrapped around mine
like i was destined to be covered in you

i saw a photo today
of you loving someone new
i forced myself to stare at it
until it didn't make me
feel anything anymore
i'm still staring

here i am
crying on the couch again
i'm so tired of getting over you

the strangest feeling
is to look at a person
you once loved
and realize
you do not know them anymore

i hate you for taking my trust from me
i can't explain how badly
i just want to be able
to love someone again

it's not the kind of sad that rips at my soul anymore frantically calling you hoping your voice will bring me back. it's the kind of sad that starts to text you, sighs, and deletes the message.

i hate that now whenever someone does something kind for me i ask myself what is in it for them.

it's not what i was expecting. after you left, you became this monster in my mind. i couldn't think about you without seeing all the ugly anger i felt. but then i see your face again and you're not a monster, you're the person i loved and that is why it hurts so bad.

sometimes the sadness makes it hard to eat. when i am so full
of emotion how can i fit anything else inside me?

candles candles candles
you always loved candles
lately all i can think about
are all the things you love
and how i'm not one of them

the only days that i can make it through without breaking are
the ones that i'm too busy to remember the pain

being stuck in your own mind
when it doesn't want to be kind
is torture
~rumination

lately all of my poems are coming out unfinished
there are times we must accept
that we exist in a world that isn't conclusive
sometimes romeo and juliet
don't fall in love
sometimes they just stop speaking
and always wonder what could have been
sometimes they meet at the wrong time
and juliet is still stuck on her ex
and sometimes they never meet at all

some people have this way
of always making themselves the victim
they twist experiences in their mind
until they convince themselves
that the whole world is against them
i am *some people*

packing up my apartment, everything makes me think of you. i know which cup in my cupboard is your favorite. i remember you teasing me while i cooked you dinner. i know exactly where i was standing in my room the first time i realized i really wanted to kiss you. i remember rearranging my room in tears the night that you didn't come home to me.

i still wish you'd come home to me.

sometimes i feel like someone's lawn
and the automatic sprinklers are on
and it's raining out
i'm drowning

"i shouldn't have trusted you"
she muttered under her breath
for what felt like the millionth time
~*the reason*

you mustn't forget that people have different methods of coping. they aren't staying away because they hate you. they just heal in a different way. you run toward people, they run away.

i don't like the idea
of hiring someone to be my friend
listening to me shouldn't be a job
~avoiding therapy

my car wouldn't start today
and it felt a little metaphorical
i'm really not going anywhere
~*stuck*

home

i can't decide which is more frightening
ending up alone
or falling in love again

it's funny to me how everyday life mixes with the internal world each of us exists in. in the notes on my phone is a mixture of my inner demons and my grocery lists. i have no idea how to trust people again, but also i'm running out of eggs. the casual needs of life mingle with the cluttered state of my mental health. i think that might be the best way i can describe life right now. i'm going to get groceries today but to me the dairy aisle isn't far from the insane asylum.

i stood out in the cold
waiting
until my tears turned into icicles
then i used them to carve your name
across my entire body
hoping
i would be able to feel you again

how do you let love in again when all it has shown you is that it is cruel, untrustworthy, and inconsistent? they say you're supposed to learn from your mistakes, but if that's true than i'm never going to let love have me again.

my biggest fear is that we were meant to be. what if we were wrong, and we missed out on all the ways we were supposed to love each other. what if timing and space was just an excuse that we used to separate two hearts that beat simultaneously. maybe we are going to live the rest of our lives watching the wrong story unfold.

she took a picture of you
sitting in a field
playing the guitar i gave you
i wonder
does she know
that we used to
sit in a field
and i would play music for you
~replaced

infinite darkness is an illusion
that your mind has created
the light
always
comes
back

whitney hanson

i see beyond your silence
you are so brave for hurting quietly

what if in my story
the protagonist fell in love
with the antagonist?
what if i don't want to fight the villain?
what if i want to invite them into my home
make them dinner and find out
what left them so broken?
what if my fight
is to make sure the villain knows love?
and although there is sacrifice in that kind of love
what if i would still choose it every time?

i can't wait for the day
that i can look into your eyes
and say
you can't hurt me
and mean it

i look at pictures of you to make myself cry
i have to keep feeling this
the alternative is scarier
feeling nothing at all
dropping into that empty pit
of not knowing what is next
seems so much worse
so i hover above the abyss
and cling to a rope i weaved
by keeping my mind in the past
but there are only
so many tears left to cry
before i must let go

i would give anything
to go back
and watch the sunset with you

in all honesty
i didn't want to see you today
i know you want us to be friends
but every time i have to see
how you have changed
into the person who no longer loves me
it breaks me again

it's been five months
and i keep telling myself
that i shouldn't feel this way anymore
but waking up without you
leaves me just as disappointed
as the first day you left

i'm convinced
that i'm feeling the hurt for both of us
because you seem perfectly fine
why do i have to carry
all of this?

whitney hanson

flowers don't feel so special
when you pick them for yourself

sometimes i feel like i'm on the outside
watching my life unfold
like it is a performance
and i'm just the audience
i'd like to consult with
whoever wrote this disaster

i know there are people who have it worse. there are some who have lost far more than what i have lost, but right now i want to be selfish with my pain. i want to pretend that you are the worst possible thing to lose because in this moment my soul aches for you and i was convinced that you were everything.

i thought running away would fix things
but i can't run away from myself
i am my biggest problem

you don't need to act tough here
hand me your hurt and i will hold you
you are safe
i am not going anywhere
anytime you need me
open this book and read these words
you don't have to be strong right now

they crawl across my body
touching all of the places
that your hands used to
they surround me
but worst of all
they weave webs
around my heart
and pull their threads
tighter and tighter
crushing me
~*spiders*

it's night and everything will feel okay again with the sunrise
trust me

flying

we don't know where we are going
but we are flying

i told you that you remind me of springtime
and i didn't lie
i just forgot that seasons are temporary
you can't tell spring to stay
the same way
you can't ask the sun not to set
but sometimes
i can close my eyes
and remember the feeling of sunlight
the smell of a fresh start
and the sound of birds singing again
thank you for reminding me
that things will be good again
even if it was only for a season

i know now that this is how it works
you don't get to keep everyone in your life forever
there are some people
that are just meant to be a sunrise for you
a light to pull you out of the darkness
there are friends, lovers, relationships
that are seasonal
and no matter how deep a conversation you had with that
person at 2 a.m.
no matter how much you shared your heart
even if you can still draw the lines of their smile
like the map of a too-familiar road
in the back of your mind
there almost always comes a time
to move on
a time to let go
and regardless of the letting go
i just wanted you to know
you're always going to feel
a little bit like home to me
no matter how temporary
it is still beautiful
that i got to call so many hearts my home

i'm beginning to realize
all we have in common now
is that i loved you once
and you loved me too

i will burn the memories of you
i will light these feelings on fire
they will fuel my flight
~*phoenix*

the sunset reminds me
every day
that not everything
you fall in love with
will last forever
you were beautiful
and you had your time
but my sky
will catch fire again
for someone new

you will find someone
that stays when you're at your worst.
you will find someone
who wants to hold you together
when you feel like you are shattered.
when you come home at 4 a.m.
they will be waiting at your door.
when your mind runs wild
and you turn into a hurricane.
they will stay
you will find someone who won't let you storm on your own.
~*patience*

the best feeling
the best feeling
was when you kissed me
and i didn't feel a thing
~healing

home

it is not selfish to tell people how you feel
what has conditioned you to believe
that expressing yourself
makes you a burden?

today i left my window open
and i let the clouds inside
they seeped into my ears
and clouded up my mind
now when the weather changes
it also changes in my head
so i always check the weather
before i get out of bed
somehow it's easier
to be told how i'm supposed to feel
this way no one can convince me
the storms in my mind aren't really real

i'd like to say the timing isn't right
but i don't believe that's true
i believe the timing was right
and we are meant to be
exactly as we are
it is not the timing that was wrong
but my idea
of what we are supposed to be
maybe we were only meant
to help each other back to our feet

if they let you go, let them go
~easy

home

i want to give you all of me
but there isn't much left
~_trying to love someone new_

nothing i told you was a lie
i was not pretending to fall in love with you
i just realized you made it way too easy
to invest my love
so i had to buy my heart back
before it became too expensive

i'm afraid that if i give out my love again
i won't be able to afford to get it back

home

it was all too heavy
i was all too weak

i think the weight of someone else
would bring me to my knees

so i'm sorry
i'd love to love you
i'd love for us to be

but i can't hold on to you
until i can hold on to me

i hurt someone else
when i was trying to fix what you broke
i tried to blame you
but i realized i *became* you

sometimes you don't get to be the victim
this time you were the one who broke someone
and i know that no one is feeling sorry for you

it's not easy being the villain

i'm not capable of loving you
the way i want to
so i'll watch you walk out the door
with all the anger i know you feel for me
clenched within your fists
this doesn't feel the best i know
but this is the best i can do

i think there is mercy
in telling someone
you do not love them

home

stop hurting your own feelings. stop walking into situations that you know are breaking you. take responsibility for your heart.

197

right now, reach over and take your own hand. realize that you are real. you are solid. you are steady. you are holding on to the one person who will never leave you, who will not walk away. fall in love with this feeling of being your own anchor.

"why are you afraid of airplanes? more people die in car crashes than airplanes."

"because if something goes wrong in a car, i may survive. if something goes wrong in an airplane, i will die."

you are an airplane
you are high risk
that's why i can't
get on board

i am in love with you
yes you
the people with fragile hearts
i think you are the bravest
most beautiful of miracles
if you cry when you read books
or if another's pain brings you heartache
if your heart cracks
for the sake of bent butterfly wings
please stay that way
do not let the weight of the world
make you hard

be loud
and colorful
and ridiculous
and don't take no for an answer

it's okay to say i miss you, but you don't deserve me. realizing that your feelings are real and cause real heartache is okay. what isn't okay is allowing those feelings to drag you around to places that are harming you. you will miss them. they were a big part of your life and a big part of you. but take a deep breath and know that you were whole before them and you are whole without them. one step at a time.

people told you to be quiet and your biggest mistake was
listening to them

i like the way she only drinks out of mugs
i like the bridge of freckles that tiptoe across her nose
i like the way she sings to make mundane tasks come alive
i like the way she values eye contact
and won't give it to you unless you've earned it
i like how she can't finish brushing her teeth
without coming up with six new ideas
to change the world
i'm in love with who she is becoming
and she is me

when i was little, i liked to do mazes. the kind on paper where you trace them with your pencil, and if you run into a dead end, you look at the big picture and find your way to the end. what i've learned as i got older, is that life isn't anything like those mazes. in life, you only get to see what's right in front of you, not the whole picture. so, when you run into a dead end, and it looks like there's nowhere to go, know that you will find your way. you will find your finish line. you just can't see it all right now.

start demanding from the universe what you are worth

i knew it was getting better when i started putting my seat belt on again. i know i shouldn't have ever stopped, but sometimes we use the value someone else gives us to determine the worth of our life.

i'm learning to take care of myself, in all the ways i wish someone else would have. anything that i longed for you to say or do, i'm beginning to realize i can do those things for myself.

i can write myself notes
i can take myself on coffee dates
i can give myself the affirmation that i need

if you're like me and you're unsure how to find that love in yourself again, set a reminder on your phone right now. type the thing you wish most for someone to tell you.

i love you.
you are enough for me.
remember to eat.
remember to wear your seat belt.

"i'm sorry" is a good reason to forgive
but silence is a good reason to forgive too

you must keep moving forward. there isn't time to hover in places that no longer serve your needs. you are not a helicopter you are an airplane and if you stop moving you will crash. disregard the uneasy feeling that looms from the unknown and take to the sky.

you're holding on to a piece of them that isn't even real anymore. that person who used to take care of your heart, that's not who they are now. it's okay to grieve the loss of who they were, but eventually the funeral has to end. you have to remember who you were before them.

you don't get to take the things i love.

i'm reclaiming the song that we called ours. i liked it before you, so it is mine to keep. i am taking back the stars. just because i admired them with you, does not mean they belong to an *us* that is dead. they still belong to me and to my heart. my favorite random parking lot, my bed, my favorite flavor of ice cream. they are all mine. you don't get custody of the things that i loved before you.

i am thrilled to be running into the unknown with every possibility ahead of me. there are hands i've yet to hold and moments when a stranger's gaze will make my heart beat at an unusual pace. there are experiences i've not yet tasted and there are places that may become home. there are sunrises i haven't seen and there is the *me* i might become.

i am terrified. i look behind me and a tear falls as i walk away from all i have known. i meet the eyes of people whom i have shared my soul with. i am leaving part of me behind. the me that fell in love with the clever man with dark eyes who taught me to play chess. there is also the me who stayed up asking her questions until 3 a.m. and the me who laid under the stars and relearned how to fall in love. there is the me whose heart was broken and there is the me who broke another's heart. i've never been good at walking away.

sometimes people are going to do really shitty things to you,
and sometimes you're going to do really shitty things to people.
and that's life darling.

constantly
colliding
with the awareness
that flowers grow best
when given space
to establish
their roots

i'm happy for you and that's how i know i'm healing

i'm going to make you a promise.
i know that scares you
and you aren't even sure
if you believe in promises anymore.

there is going to be a day
when you wake up and what they do isn't going to matter so
much anymore.
be patient

i'm beginning to realize
that it wasn't me
i was not unworthy
i was simply out of place

it isn't always going to be
the love you wanted

you've been so occupied by your hurt
that you're not sure who you are without it
existing in pain is not your purpose

i think i've healed

just kidding i can't breathe
~healing isn't linear

it may be difficult to believe
but the cold caused
by not allowing yourself to love again
is worse than the potential heartbreak
~trust issues

whoever decided that there are stages of grief and felt the need to define them can lick the bottom of my shoe. grief is not a step-by-step process. it is the ins and outs. the rising and falling of the tide. one day you feel free and the next you are sobbing into your steering wheel. you can experience anger and denial simultaneously and as many times as necessary until you heal. you *will* heal. don't allow anyone to make you believe that your emotions should be anything predictable. you are the ocean and that is how it is meant to be.

when our garden was devastated
by the fire you started
you ran to someone else
you started growing something new
i didn't start loving someone new
i stayed here for a while
i laid in the ashes
of a place that i used to feel safe
finally i walked away
with ash and seeds in my hair
i hoped to sprout roots
through my skull
a garden in my mind
that no one could devastate
because for once
the love i have is all mine

stop counting the people that have left you and using it as some kind of calculation to determine your value

i'm beginning to realize that
this has always been
about me
there wasn't anything special
about your love
that should make me crave it
the way i did
it is not so rare
that i should cry
when you gave it to someone else
it didn't hurt
because i was missing out
on something spectacular
it hurt because you didn't think
i was spectacular
and for some reason
i believed you

i never liked it when people said what's meant to be will be. i don't think there is a universal intent that has guided the way people have slipped in and out of my life. i will not credit my wins or losses to anyone but myself and the people surrounding me. to do so would be to disable my growth.

~taking responsibility

home

i want so desperately
to fall in love with the world again
i miss when strings connected my heart to the sunset
and i could hear the music that the wind played
in the space between my heart and the sun

i think if i spent as much time pondering world peace as i did thinking about someone who no longer cares about me i would have solved a lot of problems by now. that is why i'm redirecting my mental energy to things that serve others and serve me.

i'm proud of you for the things that no one has seen

i'm proud of you for getting up when you felt like it took
everything to move

i'm proud of you for not crying when you felt like you
couldn't hold it together anymore

i'm even proud of you for crying after you felt like you were
too numb and just a broken shell of a person

i'm proud of you for walking away from someone who was
hurting you so badly

i'm so proud of you

limiting your resources will allow you to get creative
don't underestimate the power of having nothing

refocus on the things
that make you feel powerful
not the people who robbed you
of your strength

i know that sadness
feels like comfort to you
but please don't stay here for too long

sometimes i have to remember to be kind with my pain. hatred doesn't need to be the product of my hurt.

"write me something beautiful," they said
so, i wrote about losing you.

"that's not beautiful," they remarked with tear-streaked cheeks.

"what is beautiful is that i survived to write about it. what is beautiful is that i broke and i'm still here. what is beautiful is that you cry with me because we both know loss. what is beautiful is that despite the emptiness i feel, tears still fall from my eyes because i am still human. what is beautiful is that losing someone is not the end of the story."

there is a kindness that i have for you that will never leave me.
no matter how badly you betrayed me.

i try to be realistic with myself
i tell myself that she is better for you
that i am healthier now alone
but that doesn't change
how badly i miss you

being lonely
is always better
than being with the wrong person
read that again

whitney hanson

some of the bruises
will last longer than others
some will hide
in your most vulnerable places
you'll forget about them
until someone says your name
a little too much like they used to

i miss the feeling of love
as if i would know what to do with it
if someone gave it to me

i stayed with sadness because she reassured me that i was capable of feeling so deeply. i ran from love because i never wanted to feel her that deeply again.

home

if you are able to acknowledge that you did something wrong and also realize that not everything wrong is your fault, that is power.

learning to thrive in stability
has not been easy for me
i have spent so long in the storm
i keep asking the sun
to bring back the clouds
why does comfort
make me feel so uneasy

if nothing else
let it be exactly what it was
mutual love for a season
a short glimpse of sunlight between the tree branches
and then you grew apart

don't hate the present
for not telling the story that you had written
after all the pen never belonged to you
the story was never yours to write
and the ending isn't your battle to fight

i hope that you're happy over there with her but sometimes i hope you look over and realize my grass is greener. i hope that sometimes you wish you had chosen differently.

interpreting emotions is hard sometimes
it's okay if you need someone else's words
to help you understand how you feel
~poetry is the language of emotion

starting over doesn't mean you have to erase every *you* that
you've ever been. you are simply changing.
growth is a good thing.

you can still cry for small things like you did when you were a child. it's okay to want something passionately and to ache when you lose it. even when that thing is just a cup of coffee you spilled on the way to work.

i bought new shampoo because i didn't want my hair to smell the way it did when i was with you. sometimes taking back the little things is important.

home

i have a habit of relocating stones
taking them from the ground
and moving them
somewhere else
sometimes miles away
it's silly
but i like to play god over rocks
it makes me feel like
i maintain some kind of control

251

i don't think they were taking you
where you were meant to go
i don't think they were
supposed to carry you anymore
as terrifying as shipwrecks are
however cold the water
may be to swim
some ships are better sunk
~capsize

i want the kind of love that is blind
but not the kind that leads me blindfolded off a cliff

thank you for saving me from settling for the wrong person by walking away from me home

the bees aren't going to go away
but they are going to change with you
sometimes they will be chaotic
sometimes they will rest
sometimes they will give you sweet honey
and sometimes they will remind you
of how much love can sting
but if you can find a home within yourself
and make peace with your bees
you will be alright

i was waiting to write this part of the book for a long time. i thought i needed to feel at home before i could write about being there. i thought i needed to fall in love. i thought that this part of the book was going to be about finding that someone who wouldn't let me go as easily as others have. i'm sorry to tell you i didn't find that. i found something else. i found that i had forgotten how to feel at home within myself. i found that i had become so far detached from myself while trying to please other people. so, i'm sorry to me. i'm sorry to the girl who used to be so passionate about life that she would wake up singing. this part of the book is for you. it's a love letter to remind you that you are whole as you are and that alone and lonely aren't always synonymous.

don't make plans to watch the sunset
it might be cloudy
watch the sunset when it catches you off guard
pause your busy life for a minute and just be still

no longer taking advice from my doubts

staring out the window of an airplane
and watching the morning sunlight touch the earth
and she whispers to me
"you belong here."
and for once
i agree with her

what are you afraid of?
name it
throw it on the ground
and step on it on your way out

no matter how you feel, your ability to see the good in everyone you meet is a gift. it is a gift that makes you vulnerable. it is a gift that will, at times, leave you on a bathroom floor crying at 2 a.m. regardless, if you always see roses and never thorns, you are extraordinary. i see how much you care and i think your heart is a garden. it is beautiful.

pick something to look forward to
even if it's really small
and please stay here for tomorrow

i tend to write about loss but i must not forget what it is to find a new home within someone else's chest. i remember when i discovered that my lips fit perfectly on yours. and although my heart no longer rests in your chest, thank you for being my temporary home.

i think the rain
is the most consistent thing
i've ever fallen in love with
the rain is the same
everywhere i have been
and everywhere i will be

there isn't this perfect destination that is out there waiting for your heart to come home to but there are places where you will find comfort and there are people who love you.

i love you.

you are afraid to love again
it feels like everyone leaves
so for now
love the things that are constant
love the sunlight
love the feeling of a soft blanket wrapped around you
engulf yourself in books
and watch documentaries about things
you've always wondered about
there will not always be someone at your side
but there will always be something to love
i promise

there is beauty in the way she holds herself that makes me hope she never allows another unworthy soul to hold her instead.

i notice even the way your fingers move
i think it is perfection
~noticing the little things about me

when your universe gets smaller
your perceived value increases
because you become more rare

so spend time alone
make your universe your own
don't overcrowd you mind
with comparison

you cannot make anyone
become enthralled with your existence
but inevitably someone will choose you
for now
choose yourself

say it to yourself:
thank you for staying

it is a privilege to love you
do not forget that

i've always been infatuated with the things most people
would call mundane
the tiny drops of water on windows after the rain
the stillness in the morning
the way each hand that i've held has felt a little bit different

i believe that the key to falling in love with life is in the tiny
movement of butterfly wings
it is two feet in the ocean feeling the sand slip from beneath
you when it is pulled by the tide

you don't have to go looking for love
you just have to be where your feet are
and breathe in the sweet air that is around you

i found myself doodling in the margins again but this time i wasn't drawing your name in a thousand different fonts. i wasn't romanticizing how lovely it looked next to mine. i wasn't squeezing our initials into hearts.

today i drew flowers and sunshine rays the same way i have since i was 10. i sketched caterpillars, butterflies, and beehives. i attempted to create the perfect star with even arms for the millionth time.

somewhere in the margins of a well-used notebook i returned to myself. somewhere between lopsided stars and beehives my heart and my hands were once again mine.

home

i made a new friend today
"dance with me," she said
i took her hand
i found that i wasn't angry anymore
"tell me your name, please"
she replied, "peace"

i cannot pretend
that i don't want someone
to fall in love with
but i know that my heart needs time
and i care for her the most

goodbye is courageous

relationships are not appraisals
do not give your heart away
for its worth to be determined
instead please
allow me to give my expert estimation
of your heart:
you are priceless

sometimes the home
you're looking for
you have to build yourself
no one knows what you need
better than you
~architect

to love yourself you must first find a new definition of love that is not the one you have learned from hurt people and failed relationships. you must learn that love is not conditional and that nothing you see in the mirror can alter the portion of love you deserve. you must learn that love is not the wage you earn for what you do or how much you do it. love is forgiving, consistent, and kind. i know that this is not the love you have learned but it can be the love you are learning.

you owe it to the world
to do those things you've dreamed of
maybe you are meant to be
someone's role model
or favorite musician
or perhaps you will write the book
that changes someone's life
but they will never hear you
if you do not speak up
if you do not become
who you are meant to be

do not speak about yourself
as if you are something small
as if there are not
whole universes begging to escape your rib cage
there is no measure of perfection
that you have to surmount
and there is no trophy
that will deem you enough
you do not have to be grateful
that you are worthy of their time
i would never wish you to be
any more
or any less

you are not alone
even the air you breathe
was exhaled by your friends
the trees

today i woke up
with happiness in my veins
tomorrow i may not feel the same
but i'm going to feel this for today

i think it is insane
the depth at which
you can care for a person
yet still neglect to care for yourself

this time—
you come first

you are so incredibly capable of collecting the stars
you just have to overcome your fear of heights

i cannot focus over the sound of all of the wonderful things
that i am meant to do

this section is titled home, not because everything is fixed and you've arrived at this destination of perfection, but because you have made so much progress and we are going to make your joy a landmark to celebrate how far you've come.

you know you are healing
when the narrative is no longer about
what they did to you
instead it is about what you are doing now

i think of my hair as a timeline
there is a part of it that grew
when i finally started to get over my ex
and part of it was the week
that i fell in love with you
my hair went with me
on our ice cream dates
and our nights under the stars
it remembers the first time i held your hand
and when i started to feel it slipping away
this is the week i spent crying in my room
this is four months i spent missing you
and the two i started working on acceptance
today i shaved my head
~*starting over*

sometimes i wonder
what's the point of all this
why do i continue to love people
when so often
we end up apart ?
i'm beginning to realize
that i am a collector of impressions
imprinting myself
with the most beautiful treasures
i have found
in the ones i have once loved
i am becoming
a mosaic of moments
a picture of joy and pain
i think that it is quite magnificent
i think that i am quite magnificent

i hope that the next person who calls you beautiful does so in a way that encompasses all of you. i hope when they call you beautiful, they mean your voice in the morning and the light in your eyes when you talk about what you're passionate about. i hope when they call you beautiful, they mean the way you forget your keys every day, so you always say goodbye twice before you leave. i hope they mean the way you sleep and the way you cry and the way you take your coffee because next time someone calls you beautiful, nothing about the way you exist should be disregarded. you are not beautiful in the way a single rose petal is you are beautiful in the way a garden is.

if you poke holes in my skin
i'm quite certain
that sunlight will spill out

i wrote her an apology
i told her
i didn't mean to fall out of love with her
i reminded her of how resilient
i believe she is
i asked her if she would take me back
~a letter to myself

she said yes

whitney hanson

recently i have realized
how important other people are.
being alone is good
but don't forget
that companionship is essential too
~*balance*

i wanted to reinvent myself. i moved to a new place. i cut off
all my hair.
i did anything to bury the person i used to be, the person that
you hurt so badly.

what i didn't realize is that i was doing exactly what you did
to her. i was reinforcing the idea that she wasn't enough. i
was trying to evade the version of myself that was suffering.
i've come to believe that change is a good thing. i don't regret
the layers i had to shed to release you.
but i refuse to forget that i live in the same skin i once died
in. i am in every way the person who fell to pieces for you.
and i am in every way the person who finally walked away.
i will change. i will grow. i will heal.
but i will never abandon myself.

if you are not unapologetically
pursuing what you love
with stardust in your eyes
please please
spend some time
talking to the sky

today i found a hole in the ground
and i thought to myself
someone must have lived there

today i found a hole in a tree
and i thought to myself
someone must have lived there

today i found a hole in an apple
and i thought to myself
someone must have lived there

today i found a hole in my heart
and i thought to myself
someone must have lived there

holes don't make us empty
they make us a home

i've been told
i wear my emotions
like a neon sign
it's no mystery how i'm feeling
so please know
if i'm glowing outside,
i'm glowing within

home

do not waste your time
trying to be beautiful
beautiful is something you already are
not something you must try to be

it is okay to want something
as long as you remain patient in your longing
there is someone out there for you
but that is not the only thing out there for you
enjoy the present

you have plenty of voices in your head telling you you're
broken and worthless. allow me to be the voice in your head
that says differently.
you are loved
you are whole
you are not alone
you are priceless

allow your smile to be young
allow your eyes to be old
enjoy life like a child
but have the wisdom to value life
as if you are on your last breath

remember how wonderful it is to go where you wish to go
and do what you wish to do.

sincerely,
independence

i think i'm on my side
it's good to have an ally

home

you will find evidence
to support anything
you choose to believe
so choose to believe you are strong
choose to believe you are capable
choose to believe you are resilient
choose to believe you belong

when you go through stormy seas
you gain an appreciation
for sailors who captain boats
on rough waters
you see people with scars from the sea
and think "they are like me"
and there we find comfort
in tracing the scars on another's skin
and knowing they have felt what you have felt
they have been where you have been

there are these things
that tug on your insides
some call them passions
i like to think of them
as the strings
that tie my soul to the universe
they remind me
that there is a reason
i am here

how to change the world:
step 1. get out of bed

my elementary school teacher asked the class
to paint a picture of the sky
all around me were papers
filled with blue skies and white fluffy clouds
my teacher looked confused at my paper
i had painted jupiter
that's when i discovered
boundaries aren't really my thing

don't be in such a rush to be someone else's
that you neglect to be your own for a while

home

your purpose is not to be what they are looking for. you are not a ball of clay to be reshaped. your purpose is to be found by the ones who discover your soul and never want to leave.

you're not going to find it. you're not going to find what you had with that person ever again. the moving on doesn't come when you find someone just like the love that you lost. the moving on comes when you accept that you're not going to relive the same love twice. you are going to find comfort in someone else's oversized sweatshirts, and you are going to make new inside jokes and laugh uncontrollably. it will never be the same, but it will be good. the moving on comes when you can be grateful for what you had and grateful for what you have.

the most beautiful people are the ones who speak with the
conviction of a thousand voices and the confidence of royalty

for so long i've needed someone to tell me
i love you regardless so i will tell it to you
i love regardless of your biggest mistakes
i love you regardless of your insecurities
i love you regardless of your past
i love you regardless of those who haven't
i love you regardless of how you've changed
i love you regardless of who you love
i love you regardless

there is no one more qualified
to fill your space in this world

you make the stars look like they are just decoration

home

there won't be this sudden moment
or profound realization
that you are beautiful
instead appreciating
your body and your self
will come gradually
it will start with thanking
your permanent home
for all she does for you
looking at the skin-colored walls
and not wishing to design them
in any other way
it will come in appreciating the way
the muscles in your face tighten and pull
to reveal your emotions
eventually
in the laughter
in your morning voice
a little at a time
you will begin to see
just how exquisite you are

i began personifying nature
i allow the wind
to run its fingers through my hair
i let the moonlight
kiss my skin
i let the rustling trees
write me poetry
i even personify the storms
i let them sweep me off my feet
and i've realized i don't need you
i never did

they gifted you the capacity to understand
all kinds of heartache
each one of them
gave you a reason to be kind to wandering souls
use this knowledge of vulnerability
to heal everyone you touch
~*past lovers*

the last person who broke my heart
gave me the opportunity to love you
you broke my heart
and gave me the opportunity to love me
~it all works out somehow

sometimes when i look at the moon
i like to imagine
you are looking too
our gaze is a bridge
from us to the sky
and there's an invisible line
that connects you and i
and even if i'm miles from you
after sunset
can we meet on the moon?
~for my someone out there somewhere

you are a force of nature
stop underestimating your ability
to command the storms in your life

i sat in the river and realized the river is not peaceful because it is still. it is peaceful because it is in motion. i am the river.

i've started to think about my life
as a long road trip
and my energy
as a tank of gas
since then, i've been more conservative
with whom i give my energy to
i'm slower to invite people into my car
i am more intentional about the places i stop
and the places i choose to rest
i have learned that my energy time and attention
are resources to be spent purposefully
most of all i have learned that movement is normal
staring at the window would be far less magical
if the car never moved
the point of the trip is that you're growing
and the point of the gas tank
is that you can be decisive
about whom you are growing with

i hope you find peace when you realize that, looking back, it's always
been the difficult times that have led you to incredible places.
your heartache is for a reason.
you are finding your way.

don't allow love to be an excuse to exist quietly. if their love muffles your voice, if it is not inspiring, if it doesn't resonate with the same intensity of sunsets and ocean waves, then know that walking away to the sound of your own marching band is the wisest path to take. allow each step to be an anthem of all of the reasons you should not be silenced.

i think it is beautiful how humanity can continue to write
about love and never seem to run out of words. it is something
bigger than all of the books can contain and it is yours
to keep
to give away
to share
to write about

whitney hanson

this morning i woke up
and she was standing by my bed
palm open to me
eyes begging me to take her hand
i closed my eyes
tried to sink back into my sadness
then opened my eyes
changed my mind
and took her hand
~_happiness_

_332_

stare at the colors in the sky
count the stars until you fall asleep
notice how warm your bed is on rainy days
so that when you lose your way you can
hold on to these moments of magic

there is this undeniable peace
in having sovereignty over one's own life
enjoy being the ruler of your own existence

you've struggled so long with that word
"belong"
you have tried to find
people and places to belong to
but people have left
and you have outgrown these spaces
the truth is
you belong to me
and to anyone else who, for a moment,
has shared your mind
or touched your soul
you belong to the sun
and to the rain
to your trials and to your joy
you have developed this misconception
that belonging is an eternal state
but you can belong temporarily
and move on when you have outgrown your home
tomorrow morning
when your feet hit the floor
please know
you belong

you don't always notice it leaving you
one day you look down and discover
that your wounds have become scars
pain doesn't usually announce its exit
eventually you just stand up
and everything
doesn't feel quite so heavy anymore

when i was writing
i felt a sense of urgency to heal
so i could finish the story for you
then i learned that the book
wasn't about the conclusion
it was about the process
home isn't the destination
it's the place where you catch your breath
get back on your feet
and continue the journey

it isn't a new beehive
it isn't a girl who held me and smelled like honey
it is me
i am home